For Grandma —

Love always,

Michelle Hasselis

W9-AHG-908

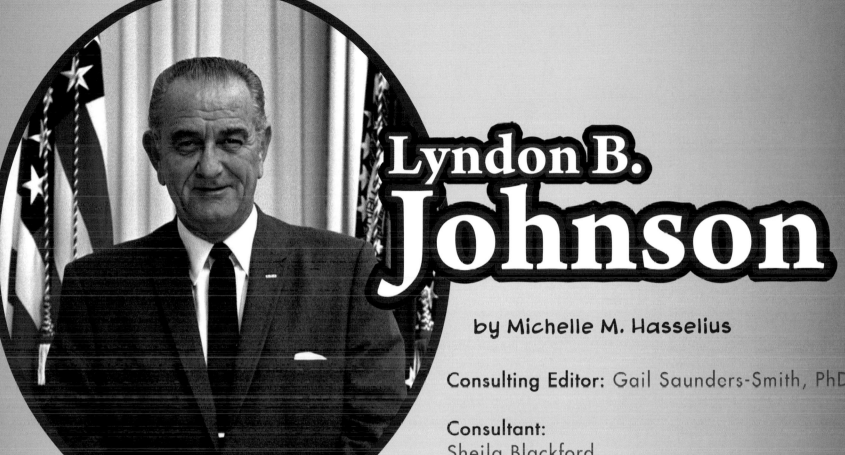

Lyndon B. Johnson

by Michelle M. Hasselius

Consulting Editor: Gail Saunders-Smith, PhD

Consultant:
Sheila Blackford
Librarian, Scripps Library
Managing Editor, *American President*
Miller Center, University of Virginia

CAPSTONE PRESS
a capstone imprint

Pebble Plus is published by Capstone Press,
1710 Roe Crest Drive, North Mankato, Minnesota 56003
www.capstonepub.com

Copyright © 2014 by Capstone Press, a Capstone imprint. All rights reserved. No part of this publication may be reproduced in whole or in part, or stored in a retrieval system, or transmitted in any form or by any means, electronic, mechanical, photocopying, recording, or otherwise, without written permission of the publisher.

Library of Congress Cataloging-in-Publication Data
Hasselius, Michelle M., 1981–
Lyndon B. Johnson / by Michelle M. Hasselius ; consulting editor, Gail Saunders-Smith, PhD.
pages cm. — (Pebble plus. Presidential biographies)
Includes bibliographical references and index.
Summary: "Simple text and photographs present a biography of president Lyndon B. Johnson"— Provided by publisher.
ISBN 978-1-4765-9611-2 (library binding)
ISBN 978-1-4765-9614-3 (paperback)
ISBN 978-1-4765-9617-4 (eBook PDF)
1. Johnson, Lyndon B. (Lyndon Baines), 1908–1973—Juvenile literature. 2. Presidents—United States—Biography—Juvenile literature. I. Title.
E847.H35 2014
973.923092—dc23
[B]   2013035448

Editorial Credits
Lori Bye, designer; Jo Miller, media researcher; Jennifer Walker, production specialist

Photo Credits
Corbis, 13; Getty Images: Time Life Pictures/Ed Clark, 11; LBJ Library photo by Frank Wolfe, 21, Unknown, 5, 7, 9, 17, Yoichi Okamoto, 19; Newscom: ZUMA Press/KEYSTONE Pictures, 15; White House Press Office: Yoichi R. Okamoto, cover, 1

Note to Parents and Teachers

The Presidential Biographies set supports national history standards related to people and culture. This book describes and illustrates the life of Lyndon B. Johnson. The images support early readers in understanding the text. The repetition of words and phrases helps early readers learn new words. This book also introduces early readers to subject-specific vocabulary words, which are defined in the Glossary section. Early readers may need assistance to read some words and to use the Table of Contents, Glossary, Read More, Internet Sites, and Index sections of the book.

Printed in the United States of America in North Mankato, Minnesota.
092013   007775CGS14

Table of Contents

Early Life

Lyndon Baines Johnson was the 36th U.S. president. He was born August 27, 1908, in Stonewall, Texas. Lyndon's family did not have a lot of money. They lived on a farm with no electricity.

born in Stonewall, Texas

1908

Lyndon at 18 months old in 1910

Lyndon went to college in 1927. He was smart and liked talking to people. Lyndon worked for his college newspaper. He was also on the debate team.

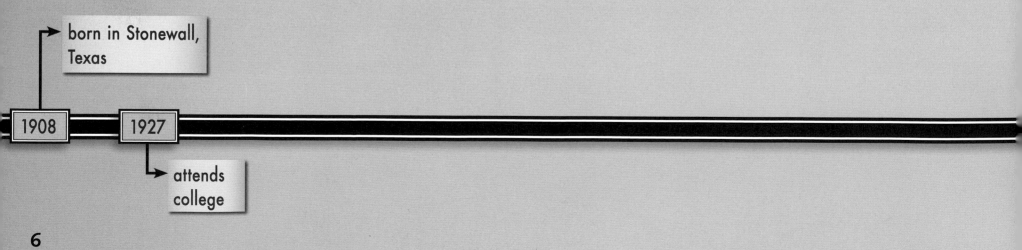

born in Stonewall, Texas

1908

1927

attends college

Lyndon in 1927

Young Adult

Lyndon worked as a teacher
during and after college.
Many of his students were poor.
Lyndon wanted to help them
make a better life for themselves.

born in Stonewall,
Texas

1908

1927

attends
college

Lyndon and his students at Welhausen School in Cotulla, Texas

5, 6 + 7th Grades
Cotulla
1928

9

Lyndon liked politics. In 1931
he worked for a congressman in
Washington, D.C. He learned
a lot about how the government
worked. Three years later
Lyndon married Claudia "Lady Bird"
Taylor. They had two daughters.

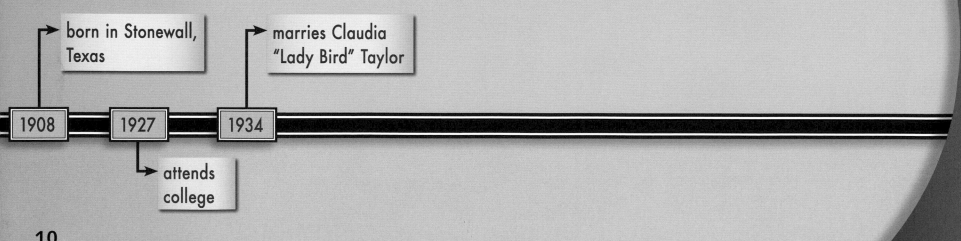

born in Stonewall, Texas

marries Claudia "Lady Bird" Taylor

1908   1927   1934

attends college

Lyndon and Lady Bird with their daughters, Lynda and Luci, in 1956

Life in Washington, D.C.

In 1937 Lyndon was elected

to the U.S. House of Representatives.

He became a U.S. senator twelve

years later. In 1961 Lyndon

became U.S. vice president under

John F. Kennedy.

born in Stonewall, Texas

marries Claudia "Lady Bird" Taylor

becomes a U.S. senator

| 1908 | 1927 | 1934 | 1937 | 1949 | 1961 |

attends college

elected to House of Representatives

becomes U.S. vice president

Lyndon and John F. Kennedy in 1961

Kennedy was shot and killed on November 22, 1963. Lyndon became the new U.S. president. Lyndon had to be a strong leader. He helped people during that hard time.

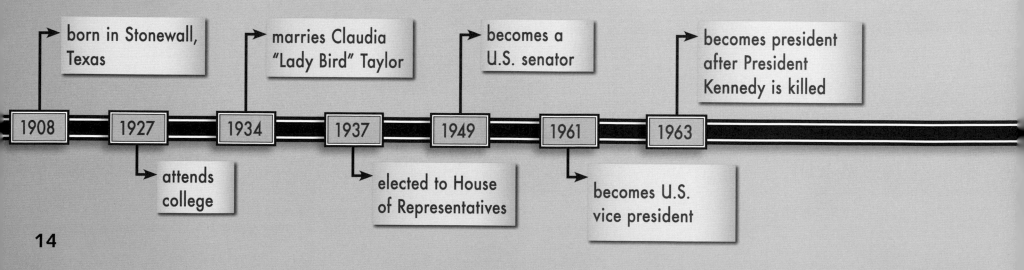

born in Stonewall, Texas

marries Claudia "Lady Bird" Taylor

becomes a U.S. senator

becomes president after President Kennedy is killed

1908 1927 1934 1937 1949 1961 1963

attends college

elected to House of Representatives

becomes U.S. vice president

Lyndon is sworn in as president
after Kennedy was killed

President Johnson

As president, Lyndon started programs to help the poor. He also signed laws that gave people equal rights. In 1964 Lyndon was elected president for four years.

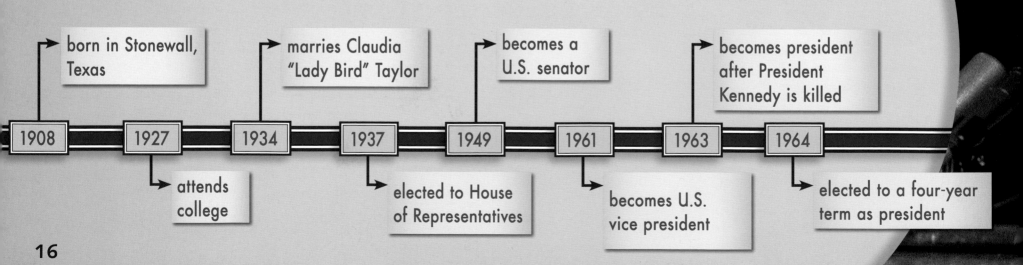

| 1908 | 1927 | 1934 | 1937 | 1949 | 1961 | 1963 | 1964 |

born in Stonewall, Texas

attends college

marries Claudia "Lady Bird" Taylor

elected to House of Representatives

becomes a U.S. senator

becomes U.S. vice president

becomes president after President Kennedy is killed

elected to a four-year term as president

Lyndon signs the Medicare Bill in 1965

Lyndon had many challenges as president. The United States was fighting in the Vietnam War (1959–1975). Many people did not like the war. Americans were also struggling over civil rights.

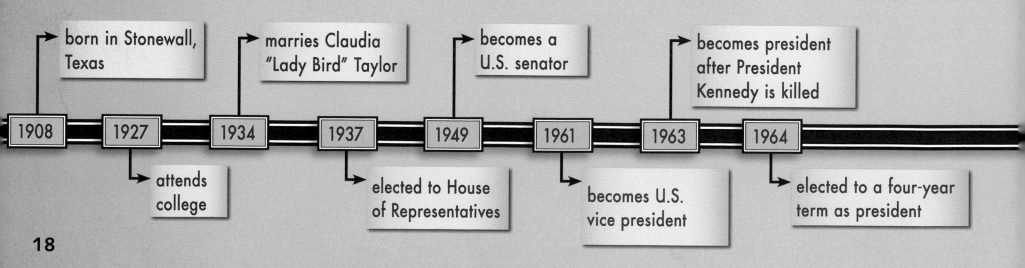

born in Stonewall, Texas

marries Claudia "Lady Bird" Taylor

becomes a U.S. senator

becomes president after President Kennedy is killed

| 1908 | 1927 | 1934 | 1937 | 1949 | 1961 | 1963 | 1964 |

attends college

elected to House of Representatives

becomes U.S. vice president

elected to a four-year term as president

Lyndon meets with civil rights leaders, including Martin Luther King, Jr. (left)

Lyndon decided not to run for president again. He moved back to Texas. Lyndon died on January 22, 1973. Lyndon is remembered for helping the poor. He also wanted equal rights for all.

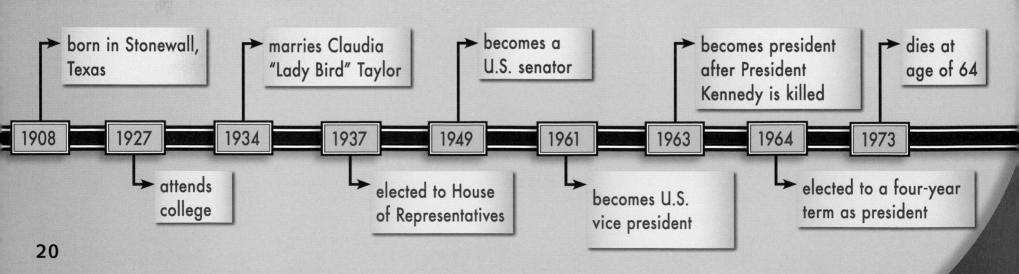

born in Stonewall, Texas

marries Claudia "Lady Bird" Taylor

becomes a U.S. senator

becomes president after President Kennedy is killed

dies at age of 64

1908   1927   1934   1937   1949   1961   1963   1964   1973

attends college

elected to House of Representatives

becomes U.S. vice president

elected to a four-year term as president

Read More

Gunderson, Megan M. *Lyndon B. Johnson.* The United States Presidents. Edina, Minn.: ABDO, 2009.

Schuh, Mari. *The U.S. Presidency.* The U.S. Government. Mankato, Minn.: Capstone Press, 2012.

Yasuda, Anita. *Lady Bird Johnson.* My Life. New York: Weigl Publishers, 2011.

Internet Sites

FactHound offers a safe, fun way to find Internet sites related to this book. All of the sites on FactHound have been researched by our staff.

Here's all you do:

Visit *www.facthound.com*

Type in this code: 9781476596112

Super-cool stuff! Check out projects, games and lots more at
www.capstonekids.com

Critical Thinking Using the Common Core

1. As president, Lyndon worked to help the poor. Describe two events in Lyndon's past that made him want to help the poor as president. Use the text and photos to help you figure out the answer. (Craft and Structure)

2. People were struggling for civil rights when Lyndon was president. What are civil rights? Describe a right you have. (Integration of Knowledge and Ideas)

3. Lyndon was on the debate team and worked on his college newspaper. What skills do you think Lyndon learned during that time that helped him as president? (Key Ideas and Details)

Index

Word Count: 272
Grade: 1
Early-Intervention Level: 23